Quotes & Such From A Lonely Traveler

Carlie Korhea Schrouder

BookLeaf Publishing
India | USA | UK

Presentation by *BookLeaf Publishing*

Web: www.bookleafpub.com

E-mail: info@bookleafpub.com

ISBN: 9789358362121

First edition 2021

To the dreamers, the travelers and everyone in between.

1. Ships That Sail

And I had no idea
when I was young
and making plans,
that the people
you start out with
do not stay

No one told me
until after the fact
that who you want
may not have a boarding pass
to where you want to go

And how vacant seats
may still hold
their carry-on baggage

2. To the Young Ones

I want to say

I am sorry that I am not often around

anymore

(but) any and every single moment that I

ever spent with you

was not just about that moment

it was about life lessons

in those small things

anytime we ever shared with each other

I was trying to pass on a life lesson of

some sort

(and) if you think really hard

you might be able to remember a few

and if you can't I just pray

that when you need it the most

one day you'll recall

what Carlie said

3. On Going

I say I'm leaving soon

you tell me "safe travels"

but never that you're coming

and never without a smile

How could my absence not move you

when the bottoms of my eyes have been

wells all day?

When it is time to go

at the turn of my heels and my luggage

wheels

I catch you bow your head

And then I know

I whisper "so long…"

And I'm sorry that I let you get

accustomed to missing me

4. Lonely Traveler's Haikus

I scan my air pass

The horizon smiles, "you've come"

My journey awaits

Window seat again

Nobody to disturb me

No one there to share

Lonely and then peace

Take up the space to my right

Landing gives me grace

5. Restless

Anyone who has ever said

to take it day by day

couldn't know how long

the days feel in your absence.

And anyone who has told me

to sleep on it does not know how

restless

I've been without you.

It's like the sun never setting.

6. Of Miles and Men

I sat with myself on a Sunday

sadness-

the saddest

And I sighed to myself

"tell me something soothing"

I sorted my thoughts and spoke

'Perhaps it wasn't the men

but the cities

that stole your heart'

I smiled at myself

It sufficed

I suppose

7. Travelling Mercies

I'm getting a plane today
she told her mother true.
Her mother said this brings me joy, for I
was rather blue.

I'm getting on a plane today
she told her sister bold.
Her sister said I wish for you
a man to have and hold.

I'm getting on a plane today
she told a friend with pride.
He said careful on your travels, dear
some people you meet may lie.

I'm getting on a plane today
she told herself so sure.
Her self said you deserve this time,

be sure to make it yours.

8. Santiago

A good traveller can plan a beautiful trip.
But a great traveller can create an
exquisite life.

9. A Traveler's Prayer

Dear God,

Before my feet lift off
the soil of this land
I say a prayer of travelling mercies
and that you'll hold my hand

I'm heading to a new place
where magic will unfold
so, I need your light to shine on me
and your divine hand to hold

Adventure bound and in search of joy
my sole companion is the view
without map or compass in sight
I find a travel guide in You

10. The Oaks

How do they make the trees here?
I know it seems like a silly question but I
need someone to tell me. Because the
leaning trees of New Orleans seem to
reach for me.
And I think it's magic- reminding me that
nature will always be the start of every
world wonder.
And I wonder what it means then;
if the leaning trees of New Orleans offer
their leaves to me.
What do they see?
Because I know they have the power to
make the world green, and the birds
sing. I mean,
they grow from dirt and sunbeams so it
means something to me.

That something that stands so

beautifully, so regally would lean

towards me.

And so, I want to know how do they

grow?

Because the leaning trees of New

Orleans are making me want to believe

that there's more to me than I see.

11. The Leaves

I watch how the leaves face the

direction of the sun and it reminds me of

a poem:

I raise my hands to the sky

Palms flat

So that everything not for me

can leave without a fight

And everything for me

can settle in with no resistance

12. Following Stars

I followed my North Node to the South

of the map

An Aquarian city greeted me from the air

and invited me to admire her waters

below

We are below sea level

I was told by a singing pianist at the

Mississippi shore

Tell me more, I wanted to ask

but the moon told me a truth that I could

not ignore

she said follow the voice of your spirit,

young traveller

it already knows what's in store

13.

Sometimes I'm scared to leave.

I think of who and what I'll miss while I'm

gone.

I worry something will go wrong.

Will the babies remember me?

When I return will they even recall my

face or the place I once held in their life

or heart?

I'm afraid to leave sometimes because

what if I don't make it home and I'm far

from everyone I know?

Whoa.

There's joy and pain in travelling for me.

When the wheels go up my heart sinks

for a split second from profound and

heavy worries

and then it returns to its place and I set

my mind on the journey.

14. A Final Request

Don't let distance be our demise.

www.ingramcontent.com/pod-product-compliance
Lightning Source LLC
La Vergne TN
LVHW050851200726
843508LV00013B/3035